IMAGES
of England

BOOTLE

The Bootle War Memorial, 1922. Erected in Kings Gardens, Stanley Road, the memorial was presented to the borough by the Memorial Committee. It was designed by Hubert Bulmer ARCA, and the figures modelled by H. Cawthra RBS. It lists all those who made the supreme sacrifice and gave their lives in two world wars. The names of those who gave their lives in other conflicts since were added later. It was unveiled my Major James Burnie MC on 15 October 1922.

IMAGES
of England

BOOTLE

Compiled by
Peter W. Woolley

TEMPUS

Tempus Publishing Limited
The Mill, Brimscombe Port,
Stroud, Gloucestershire, GL5 2QG

ISBN 0 7524 0624 8

Typesetting and origination by
Tempus Publishing Limited
Printed in Great Britain by
Midway Clark Printing, Wiltshire

RESPICE PROSPICE
ASPICE

BOOTLE.

Contents

Foreword

I was born in Bootle seventy-five years ago and have always been proud to say so. My mother taught at Bootle schools, my uncle was a local headmaster, my maternal grandfather skippered a lighter on the docks, and three generations on my father's side sailed deep-sea as Masters.

Since my start in journalism, I have chronicled the life and times of Bootle and its folk, through the '30s, the dark days of the Blitz, and the postwar resurgence as one of the leading boroughs on Merseyside.

I have been proud to have as friends many of its citizens, all of whom have cherished a pride in the town and its heritage – a pride which continues to flourish despite the area's absorption into the Metropolitan District of Sefton.

In my role of compiler of the weekly 'All Our Yesterdays' page in the *Bootle Times* I have reason to know of the deep affection people have for their town, and the affection still nurtured by ex-pats worldwide.

We all carry in our minds images of the days that used to be – of the schools, the church activities, the places of sport, entertainment and leisure, the processions and May Days, the police and the fire brigade, the factories, the shops, docks, and the memories of war and of many events, great and small.

Peter Woolley, an avid local historian, has done us a great service in presenting this excursion into the world of nostalgia selected from his collection of postcards.

Congratulations

Charles Bedford

Charles Bedford

Introduction

Respice, Aspice, Prospice – 'The Past, the Present and the Future', the motto of the former County Borough of Bootle. For over 600 years after the completion of the Domesday Book in 1086, when it was recorded that 'Four Thanes held *Botlelai* (Bootle), as four Manors', Bootle was mainly marshland, bordered by a sandy shore. Its inhabitants worked as fishermen and farm workers. Very little is recorded about this time, but trade and manufacturing were gradually introduced, and in the Census of 1810 it was revealed that there were 610 inhabitants. In the last century Bootle was a favourite seaside resort, families coming to bathe in the clean waters of the River Mersey and play on its golden sands.

When the Liverpool dock systems was spreading north and approaching the Bootle boundary, it was feared Bootle-cum-Linacre, as it was known, would be taken over by the docks and that Bootle would lose its identity. Funds were raised to purchase a Charter of Incorporation, which was granted on 30 December 1868 and brought from London. It was paraded through the streets and publicly read at the Mersey Hotel, Derby Road. Since the signing of the Charter 127 years ago Bootle has changed dramatically. The significant changes occurred after the Second World War, when Bootle was the worst devastated borough for its size in England. Bomb-damaged areas were cleared, substandard back-to-back housing pulled down, and modern houses and amenities built. The docks have played a major role in Bootle's prosperity: with the docks came the passenger and cargo ships which brought more trade to the borough.

This book portrays Bootle between 1768 and 1975 as seen through picture postcards and family photographs. Most of these have become rare collectors' items. The majority are taken from my own collection of old picture postcards collected over eighteen years. Before the First World War millions of postcards were published and posted annually, encouraged by the national craze for postcard collecting and the cheap postal rate of $\frac{1}{2}$d. The letter rate was $2\frac{1}{2}$d. Publishers like Valentines, Dennis, Frith, Salmon and Bamforths produced every imaginable subject on postcards including animals, street scenes, film stars, disasters, processions, cinemas, theatres, actors and actresses. Local photographers would produce postcard-size photographs, with a postcard printed on the reverse side to take advantage of the cheap postal rate.

Peter W. Woolley
7 Patrick Road
Bootle
Merseyside
L20 6EP

One
The Photographers

William Thomas Wright (1844-1912). He was born and raised at 26 Ash Street, Bootle. His family were staunch church-goers who attended Ash Street Mission. It is not known when he began in photography, but he must have been one of the earliest photographers in the area.

Linacre Village, 1896. This is the earliest known photograph, taken by Wright at the age of 52. He signed his photographs W. & Co. It is not clear when he started his business, which was situated in Stanley Road, next door to the Metropole Theatre. There was a photographic materials shop further up Stanley Road. He formed the Bootle Photographic Society and exhibited his photographs in and around Lancashire, winning many awards.

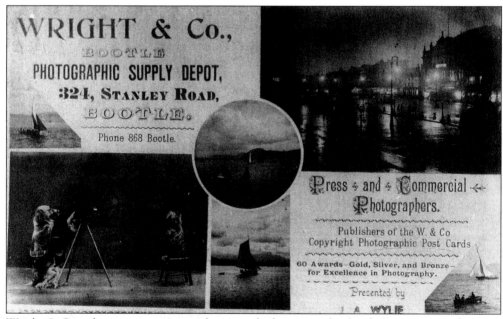

Wright & Co. advertisement. A superb postcard advertising the family business. Wright was a commercial and press photographer too. As well as producing his family studio portraits he took his equipment out and about, capturing local events.

Crosby, *c.* 1905. This winter scene is a fine example of the work he would produce.

Bridge Road, Seaforth, *c.* 1900. The Railway Hotel on the left is all that is still there today; the rest has disappeared.

Lusitania, c. 1908. This ill-fated liner was photographed at anchor in the River Mersey.

Royal Liver and Dock Offices, *c.* 1910, one of many photographs taken in Liverpool, especially around the Pier Head and the docks.

Wreck of the *Matador*, 1905. Local disasters did not escape his camera. This Russian barque went aground and broke its back at Crosby.

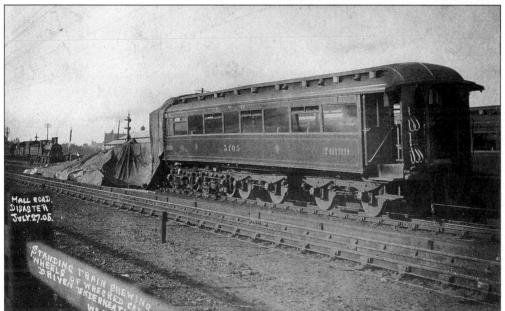

Hall Road disaster, 1905. This horrific railway disaster at Hall Road was captured by William Thomas Wright. All these photographs were on sale in his shop on Stanley Road and also seen in the local press. He died at his home on Friday 16 August 1912, and was laid to rest at Kirkdale cemetery. The business was continued until 1925 by members of his family, but the quality was not the same and the business was sold.

Percival Sutcliffe (1875-1951). His original studio was at 86 Knowsley Road, but he moved to a larger house at 457 Hawthorne Road. The living room was the studio and the front parlour was the shop. He also sold 78 rpm records, and the music could be heard coming out of the windows and open doors. He signed his photographs P.S. He later went into partnership with Terence Rigby of Knowsley Road, another local photographer. Their photographs were signed either S.R. or S.R. & T.R. His business continued until his death in 1951. There were other lesser known photographers in the Bootle area: Harry Dowden had the Parkside Studios at the corner of Stanley Road and Park Street; there was Thomas Manson of Lunt Road, and many others who did not indicate on their photographs who they were. Mention must be made of Foulds & Hibberds (Seaforth), Jeromes (Liverpool), Dorondo Mills (Carbonora, Liverpool).

Parkside Studios, c. 1910. This studio photograph was taken by Harry Dowden in his studios at the junction of Stanley Road and Park Street. The man with the lawnmower is not known. Maybe someone will recognise him?

Two
Bootle Docks

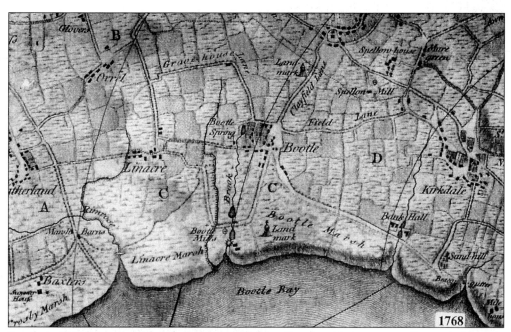

Bootle in 1768. A copy of a very early map showing Bootle and the surrounding area, Linacre, Orrel, Kirkdale, Bank Hill, Field Lane (now part of Hawthorne Road), Gravehouse Lane (Watts Lane) and Linacre Lane. Other interesting places are Sand Hill, Crosby Marsh, Glovers (now Glovers Lane), Rimrose (Road), Bootle Mills, Bank Hall, Spellow House, plus various landmarks.

Bootle landmark, c. 1790. This was on the shore near to Bootle. The reverse of this postcard reads, 'To Thomas Rodie, Esq. Vice President of the Committee of the West India Association and Senior Captain of the First Battalion of the late Regiment of Royal Liverpool Independent Volunteers, Commanded by John Bolton, Esq. This view of an Ancient Land-mark in the Township of Bootle Cum Linacre is humbly inscribed by his obedient servant, (signed) T. Troughton.

Seaforth Sands, c. 1906. Although not strictly Bootle, they shared a boundary, and the Liverpool Overhead Railway bisected the borough. This area, which includes Seaforth Sands railway station and the infamous Caradoc public house, now forms part of the Seaforth Container Terminal and Kellogs Grain Storage depot.

16

Bootle Docks, c. 1920. This aerial view shows the Gladstone Docks in the course of construction. Hornby, Alexandra, Langton and Brocklebank are some of the docks visible. The Liverpool Overhead winds its way through Bootle. North Shore Grain Terminal is prominent along with various warehouses.

RMS *Aquatania*, c. 1914. This majestic liner was the last Cunarder to have four funnels. Her maiden voyage was on 30 May 1914. She is seen here entering Gladstone lock prior to her maiden voyage.

RMS *Mauritania*, c. 1908, the sister ship to the *Lusitania* in the world's largest graving dock, Gladstone Dock, Bootle. She served as a troop ship during the First World War and returned to service with Cunard in May 1919.

RMS *Mauritania*, c. 1910. Another view of this fine ship in Gladstone Graving Dock prior to water being pumped out. The stern of this vessel shows its port of registration as Liverpool. She was sold in 1935 and scrapped the very same year.

RMS *Mauritania, c.* 1913. During the first phase of the opening of Gladstone Dock, W. & Co. took this photograph of their majesties King George V and Queen Mary inspecting the stokers aboard this vessel.

HMS *Rodney, c.* 1942. Built at Cammell Laird, Birkenhead, in May 1922, she was involved in the search and eventual sinking of the German pocket battleship the *Bismark* in May 1941 whilst under the command of Captain Dalrymple-Hamilton. She is seen here in Gladstone Dock on a courtesy visit to Bootle.

Cunard liner *Saxonia, c.* 1905. In its day it had the tallest funnel. At the start of the First World War she was used as a German prisoner-of-war ship moored in the Thames. A tug is assisting her into Hornby Dock, Bootle.

Dock bobbies, *c.* 1953. Two of the Liverpool City Police Force Dock Division. Constable '61E' (on the left) is wearing one war service medal ribbon. Constable 2nd class (denoted by the two inverted chevrons) 167E has war medal ribbons up and a long service medal ribbon denoting at least twenty-two years service. Both uniforms have only two pockets; this later changed to four. The uniform jacket has the stand-up collar which went out in the mid-50s. The photograph was taken at Hornby Dock with a Cunarder behind.

Hornby lighthouse, c. 1905. Known locally as the 'Bootle Bull' because of the deep resonant sound made by its fog horn, it stood on the north wall and was demolished in 1928 to make way for a new lighthouse at Gladstone Dock.

AEC lorry, *c.* 1930. Various types of vehicle plied their trade on the dock estate. This AEC lorry is seen at Hornby Dock with its driver after being loaded with Canadian hams. It is owned by J.C. Transport Company, Liverpool.

North Shore Mills, 1911. This grain storage warehouse, situated in Strand Road, was photographed from Regent Road. This building and other prominent Bootle landmarks were used by the German Luftwaffe during bombing raids on Bootle and the docks during the May blitz. The Strand public house in Strand Road, used for many years by the Bootle dock workers, has recently been modernized and renamed the Wobbly Duck.

RMS *Lusitania*, *c.* 1908. This majestic liner was built for the Cunard Line. It is photographed being manoeuvred into Langton lock with eight tugs in attendance, to the delight of the crowd that throng the quayside. This ill-fated liner was sunk by German U-boat U.20 off the Old Head of Kinsale, southern Ireland, on 7 May 1915.

Langton Dock, *c.* 1905. A busy dock scene, with a tug towing a tree-masted vessel *Atlantic*, registered in Stavanger, Norway, towards Langton Lock. As she left the Mersey, she hit a storm, went aground at Southport and broke her back. This is the last photograph to be taken of this vessel, taken as it was on the day of the storm. The tugs are, left to right: *Langton*, *Victoria*, and *Toxteth*.

Langton Dock, c. 1908. A busy day at the dock. Part of the hydraulic pumping station's clock tower was a victim of the Luftwaffe. The pump-house keeper was a Mr Petrie, who lived there with his wife. Completing the picture are merchant ships, sailing barges, gig-boats, tugs and water tenders.

SS *Baltic*, c. 1909. Bootle dockers are seen carting beef from this White Star Line vessel and loading it into a container owned by Aldersons Depository in Church Street, Bootle. The team of horses belong to Thomas Wilson, Berry Street, Bootle.

Three
Bootle Borough

Bootle Hot Pot Fund, 1910. In Millers Bridge in the borough itself there was a public bake house, to which the poor could take dough wrapped in pillow cases to make their bread. Each Christmas a Mr John Simpson, butcher, would provide small bowls of hotpot to be distributed free to the poor and needy of the area. The Mayor and Mayoress of Bootle, James R. Barbour, J. Simpson, a councillor and PC 54 complete the picture.

St Johns Road, Bootle, *c.* 1915, typical terraced housing in the Bootle area, near to the docks. Numbers 9, 11, 13, 15, 17 and 19 are shown. Malcolm Street is to the right.

St Alexander's church, *c.* 1912. Situated in St Johns Road, just on the Bootle boundary with Kirkdale, this was the church of Teresa Higgins, who was reputed to have stigmata on her hands and feet which were said to bleed at various times. She was buried at Neston on the Wirral, and many still believe she should be canonized.

Bootle multiview, c. 1924. Five views of Bootle: the municipal buildings and the Town Hall, Oriel Road; Merton Road; Stanley Road; War Memorial, Kings Gardens, and (circled) the Band Station in Derby Park.

Bootle multiview, c. 1905. An earlier multiview, with Stanley Gardens, Derby Park rustic bridge, Town Hall, Merton Road-Litherland Road junction, and the Stanley Road-Strand Road junction.

Oriel Road, Bootle, *c*. 1908, looking from the direction of Oriel Road railway station entrance towards Merton Road. All these houses have gone to be replaced by modern office blocks.

St Catherine's Road, *c*. 1902. Photographed from Oriel Road looking towards Pembroke Road, these one time fine houses were the homes of well-to-do Bootle citizens. Many have been converted into flats and nursing homes, although a few are still private residences.

Bootle Times offices, *c.* 1905. Backing onto Oriel Road railway station, and close to the station entrance, this was the second print shop and offices, the first being in Balliol Road. It remained there until 1963, when the *Times* moved to Bootle New Strand. The building was eventually vandalized, set on fire, and demolished.

Bootle Railway Station, *c.* 1910. This is one of four stations that existed in the borough. It was opened in 1876 alongside Oriel Road, and was an intermediate station on the line between Liverpool (Exchange) and Southport (Chapel Street) for the Lancashire and Yorkshire Railway.

Oriel Road Station, *c.* 1951. Six years after World War Two, Bootle was getting the borough sorted out after the bombing. Oriel Road railway station looks drab and in need of a coat of paint. Johnsons Dye works is in the distance.

Oriel Road, *c.* 1910. The railway station canopy fronts Oriel Road. The Wyndham Hotel is opposite, with the shops of Mrs Mary Wright, confectioner (No. 45), William B. Heywood, (No. 47), R.W. Hall and Co., coal merchants (No. 49), Mrs Mary Jane Houghton, stationers and tobacconists (No. 51), and Thomas H. Swinton, chemist.

30

Trinity Road, *c.* 1910, taken from Oriel Road, showing Bootle Town Hall with its ornate lamps. At the very top on the right is Trinity church. The houses to the immediate left have gone and now form part of the Town Hall car park. The apex-fronted houses are the only ones left up to Stanley Road; the others, and the church on the left, have all gone and this is now part of the commercial centre of Bootle.

Bootle Town Hall, *c.* 1910. Opened in 1882, this was the heart of the administrative side of Bootle, and also the offices and parlour of the Mayor and Mayoress of Bootle.

Bootle Town Hall, *c.* 1910. This impressive building, extended in 1902, also contained the Borough Museum and Library. Further down Oriel Road is Trinity Road.

Bootle Town Hall, *c.* 1910. The Mayor of Bootle, Hugh Carruthers, is standing on a raised platform outside the Town Hall in front of a packed Oriel Road, reading out the Proclamation of King George V's accession to the throne.

Military ceremony, *c.* 1914. The scene in Oriel Road during preparations for handing over the colour of the Liverpool Kings Regiment into the care of the borough before they enter the European war. Top left is North Shore Mills, and behind the trees is the premises of George Williams, joiner. Some of the houses are still there, mainly turned into flats.

Military ceremony, *c.* 1914. The guard of honour formed up outside the Town Hall in Oriel Road. An officer carries the colour to be presented. On the right is the booking office of Balliol Road railway station.

Military ceremony, c. 1914. The colours of the Liverpool Kings Regiment (Bootle) are presented to the Borough of Bootle for safe-keeping until the regiment returns from World War One.

Oriel Road-Balliol Road, c. 1920. The main Post Office was at this junction until it moved to larger premises in the New Strand. Later it was part of South Sefton Magistrates Court, until the new courts were built at the junction of Stanley Road-Merton Road.

Balliol Road, *c*. 1908, an early view looking towards Stanley Road. Notice the gas lamps and the trees in tubs lining the road. On the left is Bootle Baths and Gymnasium, which opened in 1888. It had a salt water pool for men and another for women, and also boasted Roman, hot air, Vapor and other private baths and facilities.

Technical School, *c*. 1904. Established at the Free Library in 1881, until this one was built in 1890, this institution included a School of Art and secondary school for boys which was opened in 1901.

Wesleyan chapel, *c.* 1903. Standing at the junction with Pembroke Road, the Balliol chapel (Wesleyan Methodist), opened in 1866 and could accommodate 900. Sadly, it is one of the many Bootle churches that are no longer with us.

Emmanuel church, *c.* 1903. This Congregational church at the junction of Stanley Road and Balliol Road was opened in 1876. The tower was added in 1908. Although damaged during the May blitz, it survived the war but fell foul to vandals and was burnt down in the early 1960s.

Stanley Gardens, c. 1904. The gardens were given to the town by Lord Derby. The king's statue was given by Colonel Sandys and was unveiled by him in the presence of Lord and Lady Derby. The postcard show the statue after it was unveiled. South Park is to the rear of Stanley Gardens, with Hawthorne Road and Balliol Road also in the picture.

The king's statue, c. 1904. This photograph was taken after everyone had gone home from the unveiling ceremony. It shows King Edward VII resplendent in full coronation robes.

Stanley Road, *c.* 1908. A senior citizen muses with his pipe whilst Bootle life passes before him. I wonder what tales he could tell about the old Bootle? Emmanuel Congregational church is minus tower, which is in the course of construction. The house next door was once a Corporation hostel for the blind. It is now nursing home, Connolly House.

Stanley Gardens, *c.* 1919. Later renamed Kings Gardens, this elevated view shows off its beautifully laid out gardens. Off Stanley Road are Hertford Road and Exeter Road, where the works of John Geraghty, stone mason, were renowned locally for head stones and monuments. The large house at the junction with Balliol Road later became the Bootle School of Art.

Exeter Road, c. 1907. To the left is part of Geraghty's yard, and a fine row of terraced houses. The message on the reverse of this postcard reads, 'My dear Nell, Another for your postcard collection. I thought you may like to see how your domicile looks on a picture postcard.' (It was signed 'M').

Wadham Road, c. 1906, taken from Stanley Road, looking towards Queens Road and the railway. The yards on the left at Nos 82 and 84 were owned by John Cothliff, slater, plasterer and general contractor.

Stanley Road, *c.* 1915. The entire staff of the City of Liverpool Equitable Co-operative Society Ltd, branch No. 27, pose for the camera. Even a lady in the flat above gets into the act. It was situated on the corner of Wadham Road. A sign in the window is a First World War sugar rationing poster.

Bedford Road, *c.* 1908, seen from Miranda Road, looking up Hawthorne Road. How clean the streets looked without cars! All the houses had the same type of early Venetian blinds in all the windows. The Hawthorne pub is visible in the mist, at the junction with Hawthorne Road.

South Park, c. 1912. Another incorrectly titled postcard. The public shelter near to the Balliol Road entrance was a meeting place for local senior citizens, who would while away the time spinning yarns about 'The Good Old Days'. Some of the fine houses in Balliol Road are behind the shelter.

Balliol Road, c. 1905. Tree-lined Balliol Road with its cobbled road surface and fine houses makes for a lovely picture. South Park is to the right. The large house which stood in Hawthorne Road was Quarry Bank, owned by the Revd Stanley Rogers.

Hawthorne Road, *c.* 1912, looking towards Balliol Road, and showing the fine home of Silas Locke, a local house builder. This lovely house was destroyed in the May blitz and was never rebuilt. Across Balliol Road is Trinity church, on the corner of Trinity Road.

Breeze Hill, *c.* 1913. The wall on the left is Christ Church vicarage on the Worcester Road. Among these large houses were an Auxiliary Military Hospital, Miss Turner's Dancing Academy, and Blair Gowery, which was private school. The large house at the top right was later replaced by the Mons Hotel.

Blair Gowery, c. 1953. Some of the schools pupils are seated in the rear garden enjoying a party to celebrate the coronation of Queen Elizabeth II.

THE MONS HOTEL, BOOTLE.

The Mons Hotel, c. 1967. Built in 1966, it was named after the Belgian town of Mons, with which Bootle was twinned.

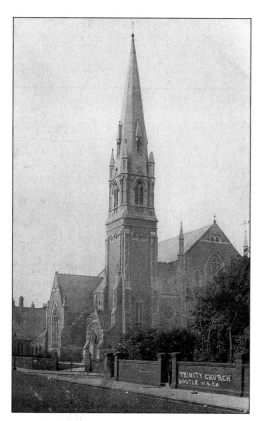

Trinity church, *c.* 1907. St Paul and Trinity was constructed in Hawthorne Road at its junction with Trinity Road in 1887. This spire of his beautiful church was damaged during the May blitz and removed as it was unsafe, but the tower remained. Due to deterioration of the brickwork and woodwork it was decided to demolish it. In 1984 sheltered housing accommodation was built on this site.

A snow-covered Breeze Hill, *c.* 1906, with Christ Church shrouded in winter mist. It was built in 1866 by Dove Bros. after a design by R.H. Carpenter & Slater. William Thomas Wright took this photograph.

Christ Church, *c.* 1904. Interior view showing the Corinthian-style columns and the use of different shades of brickwork. The main stained glass window were damaged during the war, and remaining fragments were incorporated in the new window.

THE OLD HALL, BOOTLE.

The Old Hall, *c.* 1979, No. 1 Merton Road, as it is today. This building is reputed to have been the shooting lodge of Lord Derby in the eighteenth century. It is thought that he brought some of his friends to shoot grouse, partridge, deer and wild boar on Bootle marshes (Marsh Lane) and forests. Merton Road was also the home of Samual Walters, a marine artist of considerable fame throughout the world. He also built the Staniland Villas, Merton Road in 1873. Many of the houses in the area were built by wealthy merchants and businessmen.

Bootle village, *c.* 1911, located in Litherland Road at the junction with Park Street. Very few photographs of the village are known to exist. A well-to-do couple stands at the junction of Litherland Road and Merton Road, where this photograph was taken. The shops include, left to right: the Bootle Circulating Library and Sweets and Tobacconists, Edward Turpin, family butcher, George Lunt, bakers, Gilbert Mathews, boot repairer, and the Jawbone Tavern (John Pennington, licensed victualler), which got its name from the jawbone of a whale which hung inside the vestibule door. Bootle village can just be seen beyond Park Street.

No. 7 Merton Road, *c.* 1911. This imposing house stands at the junction of Litherland Road and Merton Road, and was named Carlton House. It was owned by a William H. Green, a manager. This fine house still stands today and is an imposing sight.

Thomas Scott, c. 1910. This family group was taken in the rear garden at 46 Merton Road, the family of Thomas Scott, bakers. Thomas is the one standing at the rear.

SCOTT'S EMPIRE BAKERIES

THE HOME OF GOOD BREAD

Scotts Empire Bakeries, c. 1962. This aerial view was taken at the Netherton bakery. Although not in Bootle, it became part of Bootle during boundary changes. Dunningsbridge Road is in the foreground. The bakery closed in the 1970s, although part of it is now used by a smaller bakers. The majority of the site is now a retail park.

MERTON ROAD & STANLEY ROAD, BOOTLE,

Merton Road-Stanley Road, *c*. 1929. At the top of Merton Road is Christ Church, and on the right hand corner behind the tram-car was a Military VD Hospital for the American servicemen billeted in the area. After the war it became the Merton Hotel. On the left hand corner opposite the hospital was a doctor's surgery which was demolished. Years later South Sefton Magistrates Court was built on this site.

STANLEY ROAD, BOOTLE.   B.I.

Stanley Road, *c*. 1950. Near to the junction with Merton Road stood the Stanley Road Baptist church, established in 1846 and opened in 1897. To the right of the church stood Morton Gardens. Sadly, both of these are no more. This site is now occupied by St Johns House, owned by the Inland Revenue. Plans have been drawn up to have this building demolished.

STANLEY ROAD — BOOTLE

Stanley Road, *c*. 1908. The Bootle Reform Club House Co. Ltd, Arthur Watson, Chairman, J. Mohan, Secretary (Hons), Thomas Cooke, Manager. It stood to the left of the tram stop. Photographer Harry Dowden had his Parkside Studios at the corner of Park Street, Stanley Road.

STANLEY ROAD, BOOTLE.

Stanley Road, *c*. 1928. The Bank of Liverpool is just visible (left) with the shops of Mrs M.S. Benjamin Cain, butchers, John Hughes, grocer, who advertises 'Joy of Home Tea' above his shop, Harold Wyatt, chemist, and Armstrong & Co., confectioners.

A winter scene, Stanley Road, *c.* 1907. No. 204 is Harry Dowden, photographer; No. 206 (on the corner of Park Street) is Geo. Parr, plumber. The prominent building was A.B. Spencers, manufacturers of the famous 'Spenso' and 'Sweet Nell' beverages and the famous 'Aunt Sally' disinfectant. On the side wall is an advertisement for the Muncaster Theatre.

Gilbert Norris's, *c.* 1908. No. 232 Stanley Road was the first van offices for Gilbert Norris, Removals. This postcard shows Mrs Gilbert Norris outside the office with her son Jack and her daughter-in-law. Note the old type of Venetian blinds.

Stanley Road, c. 1933, at the top of Sullivans Brow, on the canal bridge. J.C. Nichol was manager of Parr's Bank Ltd. Shops included a confectioners, estate agent, Stanley Tailors (merchant tailors), A.B. Starmore, postcard printers. On the left is one of the well known police boxes, No. 3 Box. Barclays Bank was next to it. A Ribble bus drives over the tram lines of Liverpool Tramways routes 16, 28, 23 and 24.

Stanley Road, c. 1929. Johnsons Dyers, at No. 267, was next to the outfitters shop, No. 269, owned by Mrs Mary Beaumont, which has been decorated either for a royal occasion or one of Bootle's May Day celebrations. No. 271 was Henry John Bettesworth.

Stanley Road, *c.* 1906. A Bootle bobby stands on point duty at the junction with Strand Road. The Lancashire and Yorkshire Bank (now Kwik-Save) stands on the corner; James Walsh, hairdresser, was at No. 290. Next door was Potter Brothers, pawnbrokers. Miss Alice Joy, wardrobe dealer, and Rannard Longworth & Co. Ltd, varnish and paint manufacturers, are just some of the identifiable shops. On the left is the Langton public house. The advertising hoardings to the right of the trams mark the site of the proposed Metropole Theatre which was built in 1910-11.

Stanley Road, *c.* 1914. A superb photograph taken prior to 1914 of this busy junction. A Blackledges delivery cart stands outside the shop, with Boots Cash Chemists next door. The Langton pub is on the corner of Strand Road. Tram no. 68 is on route to the Old Haymarket via Byron Street. The advertisement on the front is for Casket cigarettes.

Railway strike, *c.* 1911. In August 1911 the railway workers at Brunswick Dock went on strike when their employers refused their pay claim. All workers in Liverpool, Bootle and surrounding areas supported the strike, and the city and all transport came to a standstill. Casual labour was brought in which further inflamed the already volatile situation. Troops were mobilized and policemen from neighbouring forces were sent to assist in the guarding of goods, rioters and prisoners. W.&Co. took this picture of police and troops marching from Stanley Road into Strand Road.

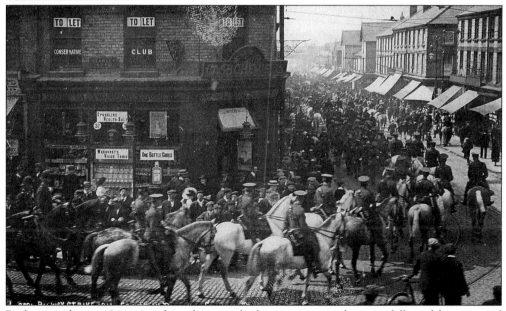

Railway strike, *c.* 1911. Another photograph showing mounted troops followed by mounted police turning into Strand Road passing Boots Cash Chemists, above which is the Conservative Club which is To Let. Local people lined the route, shouting abuse at the police and troops.

Strand Road, *c.* 1907. No. 204 Strand Road, on the corner of Cedar Road, was the family home of Charles Cowell, shopkeeper, and some of the family pose for the camera. It is not known where the Cowell shop was, or what type of shop it was.

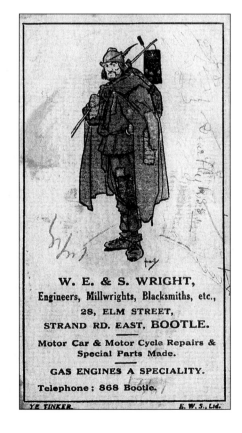

W. E. & S. WRIGHT,
Engineers, Millwrights, Blacksmiths, etc.,
28, ELM STREET,
STRAND RD. EAST. BOOTLE.

Motor Car & Motor Cycle Repairs &
Special Parts Made.

GAS ENGINES A SPECIALITY.

Telephone : 868 Bootle.

YE TINKER.   E. W. S., Ltd.

W.E. & S. Wright advertisement, *c.* 1906. This is an ink blotter advertising the firm of engineers, millwrights and blacksmiths. Their premises were at 28 Elm Street. These blotters were given away to business clients.

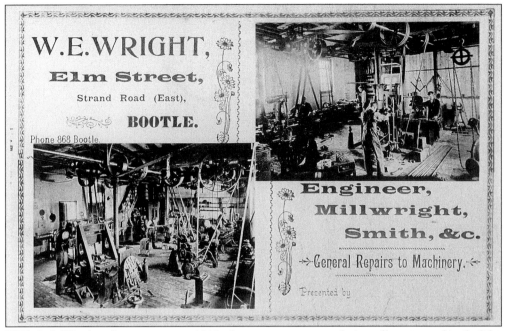

W.E. & S. Wright advertisement, *c.* 1911, this time on a postcard. As well as giving detail of the firm it also included two photographs of the workshops.

A. Wright, motor haulage contractors, *c.* 1920. This vehicle was a Clayton Shuttleworth, model no. 47393, and its registration number was FE 1878. This vehicle has been especially adapted for taking local children out for the day.

A. Wright, motor haulage contractors, *c.* 1918. Another fine vehicle, again adapted for taking out children possibly from Ash Street Mission. Note the solid tyres. Arthur Wright is third from the right.

A. Wright, motor haulage contractors, *c.* 1910. It is possible that Arthur Wright owned this trailer and hooked it up to one of the aforementioned lorries. It must have made a lovely sight, with all the kids shouting, and being sick, what with the solid tyres on cobbled roads!

John Wolfenden, dairyman, *c.* 1930. The dairy which he ran with his two sons, Kenneth and John, was at no. 1 Beech Street. John Wolfenden is taking a break from deliveries in what is believed to be Trinity Road. Milk was sold by the jug at the dairy.

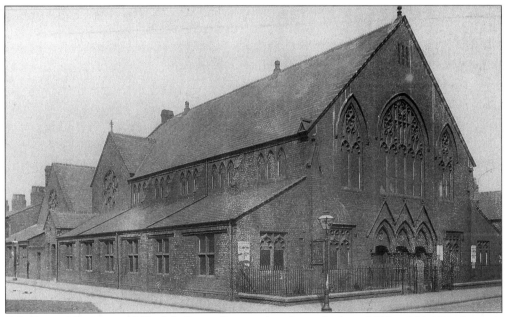

Ash Street Mission, *c.* 1905. Ash Street Baptist church was built in 1886, within Bootle-cum-Linacre, at the junction of Litherland Road. Prior to its being built services were held at premises in Bootle village, New Street (off Linacre Lane), and Waterworks Street.

Ash Street Mission, *c.* 1925. This interior view of the Mission was taken by W.&Co. who belonged to this church. To the left of the organ is a marble tablet in remembrance of Joshusa William Schofield, founder of the young men's Bible class. On the organ's right is a marble tablet to the memory of Robert James Glasgow, founder of the Mission in 1863.

Ash Street scouts, *c.* 1925. The 7th Bootle scout troop was based at Ash Street Mission and was formed in 1924. The scout master for many years was Mr W.E. Wright, the brother of W. & Co., photographer, and Sydney Wright, artist and sculptor.

Linacre men's Bible class, c. 1910. This fine body of men was photographed in the garden at the rear of the home of a Mr Hanlon (Hanlon Avenue was named after him) at Breeze Hill, Bootle. Sixth from the right in the second row is Joshua Schofield and seventh is Robert Glasgow. On the very front, leaning on his arm, is William Thomas Wright (W. & Co.). First right in the second row is Mr Wright snr.

E.G. Stevenson, haulage contractor, c. 1939. The vehicle is a Foden diesel, registered number AYS 316, seen here in Vermont Street, off Delaware Street. The wire hawsers stacked on it were used in the lifting of the ill-fated submarine *Thetis*. Mr Stevenson is in the centre of the group.

Advertising postcard, c. 1911. This is the type of postcard that was used by numerous firms to advertise their goods. Appleby's Flour Mills were no exception. The mills which backed onto the canal used it to transport flour to and from Bootle Docks.

Foden lorry CJD 256, c. 1960. This vehicle of B.I. Transport Co. Ltd. is seen here parked up whilst working at Appleby's Flour Mills. This vehicle was formerly owned by Joseph Rank Ltd.

Applebys Flour Mills, *c.* 1937. Appleby's own football team at the end of the 1936-37 season, when they were the Business House League winners. They won the J.V. Rank Championship Cup and were also finalists in the League Cup.

Strand Road, *c.* 1915. The No. 23 tram has just turned left from Stanley Road and is approaching the passing loop section of the single line working of the tram lines. Among the shops shown on this postcard are Salter & Salter (1900), boot factors, Maypole provisions, Ransons, drapers, Pegram, grocers, Chas. White, fish dealer, and the British and Argentine Meat Co. Ltd.

Strand Road, *c.* 1918, looking in the opposite direction towards Strand Road railway station and the docks. The streets around Strand Road were given American names, i.e. Boston, Carolina, Delaware, Garfield, Jersey, Nevada, Oregon, Orlando, Vermont, Virginia and Washington Street.

Strand Road Fire Station, *c.* 1902, built in that year to replace the old fire station close to the docks in Strand Road. This building cost £35,000 and had a permanent staff of twenty-five and an auxiliary staff of twenty-five. There were four steam fire engines, two horse hose tenders and five fire escapes. After many years faithful service it closed in 1979.

Bootle fire chief, c. 1927. The coffin of Cecil Monk is carried on a Bootle fire engine. The funeral took place at St Mary's church, Bootle. The photograph shows the cortège in Church Street, about to enter the church. Walking in front is Station Officer Mark Eady, who later died in tragic circumstances in the line of duty, as did Cecil Monk.

St James church procession, c. 1911. The procession is seen passing the Muncaster pub and the Muncaster Theatre in Irlam Road. The Royal Muncaster Theatre was built in 1890 and was also named the New Princes Theatre. Apart from variety, it also showed films and was known locally as the 'Ranch House' on account of the large number of westerns shown. It was said that if you did not have fleas when you went in, you certainly had them when you came out!

Theatre advertising, *c.* 1910. A handbill of the type that was given to patrons as they left the theatre, this one for the Muncaster Theatre, Bootle. Issued for the Jubilee celebrations, it shows two performances on 22 June, at 7.30pm and at 10.30pm. I wonder when second house ended?

The Metropole Theatre, *c.* 1912. Bootle's favourite, it was built in Stanley Road and opened in March 1911. Sadly it was destroyed during the May blitz. Its site is now occupied by an amusement arcade, Chinese restaurant, fruit shop, and a firm of solicitors. Opposite is the Triad building.

J. FORBES KNOWLES and HARRY MASTERMAN'S CO.

TEMPLE IN THE GROVES OF MANDALAY

IN A . MAN'S POWER

By ARTHUR SHIRLEY and BEN LANDECK.

Enthralling Story !

Brimful of Comedy

Elaborately Mounted !

Strong Woman Interest

Theatre advertising, *c.* 1912. *In a Man's Power,* on Monday 30 June for six nights, is the play advertised on this postcard for the Metropole Theatre.

Hetty King, *c.* 1916. Many famous variety acts cut their teeth on the boards of the Metropole and returned time after time. One such artist was Hetty King, the male impersonator. She had many well known songs to her credit, including *All The Nice Girls Love A Sailor.* This autographed postcard is believed to have been signed at the 'Met' stage door.

Marie Lloyd, c. 1909. Another performer popular with Bootle audiences. Her real name was Matilda Wood, and she was born in London in 1870. A true cockney, she introduced many saucy songs and themes to the variety stage. She was famous for extravagant costumes. One of her favourite songs was *The Boy I Love Sits Up In The Balcony*. Marie was married three times and died in 1922.

Wolstenholmes Florists, c. 1920. This lovely shop-front was at 343 Stanley Road, almost opposite the Metropole Theatre, from which it derived a lot of business either decorating the theatre or selling flowers for the artistes.

Temperance march, c. 1905. This demonstration, campaigning on the evils of alcoholic beverages, took place through the streets of Bootle. Most of Bootle's churches were marching, including the Welsh Chapel from Marsh Lane, as can be seen from the banner. The march has just passed the advertising hoardings behind which would be built the New Metropole Theatre in Stanley Road. Aldersons Depository and Furniture Warehouse are visible.

Stanley Road, 1905. Aldersons Depository, John Rafter JP, physician and surgeon, and the Lancashire and Cheshire Billiard Hall are the buildings to the immediate right up to the corner of Ash Street.

Stanley Road, c. 1905. An early view of Liggetts Pioneer Store at 344 Stanley Road, with staff and customers posing for the photographer. Note the large number of biscuit tins in the doorway and the wide variety of goods for sale in the window.

Stanley Road, c. 1920. A later view of the same shop, with a profusion of meats hanging from hooks on the exterior of the shop. This time just the staff are posing for the camera. Ash Street is just visible to the right with the chimney of Pine Grove above the rooftops.

Stanley Road, *c.* 1931. Birch & Co., high class confectioners, were at 407 Stanley Road, with the chandlery store of Mrs Martha McClure to the left and Thomas F. Riley, butchers, to the right.

Marsh Lane, *c.* 1910. The Wesleyan chapel was a unique church inasmuch as it stood between two public houses. On the left can be seen the side wall of the Jolly Farmers, and to the right the Railway Hotel. This was one of the buildings destroyed in the May blitz.

Bootle Concertina Band, *c*. 1932. The band is seen here forming up in Smyna Road, off Malta Road, in readiness for one of the May Day parades.

Welsh Chapel, *c*. 1906. A young lad stands on the corner of Cyprus Road and Marsh Lane, outside the Welsh Chapel, looking rather puzzled. This is another church that has long gone. North Park can just be seen at the top of the road.

St James, c. 1906. This beautiful church in Chestnut Grove was erected in 1845 and re-erected in 1866. It could accommodate 900 persons. The photograph was taken to commemorate the Golden Jubilee of Canon Kelly.

St James, c. 1906. The lovely interior, including the high altar and the superb reredo below the main stained glass window, is captured by the camera.

Littlewoods Pools, 1950. The Bootle branch of this famous Liverpool firm was situated in Irlam Road. This photograph shows a prize-winning netball team being presented with their trophy by Mr Woods (branch manager).

Salisbury Road School, c. 1920. All the schools in the borough had their football teams. Salisbury Road School were league champions in the 1919-20 season. What are their names? Somebody must know.

St James, 1913. The mace bearer leads the Mayor John Rafter and other civic dignitaries towards the church.

Marsh Lane, 1907. The Day Industrial School was built in 1895 at the junction with Irlam Road (where the Brunswick Boys Club now stands). It was built to meet the social needs of poor local families, and continued in this capacity until 1914.

Marsh Lane, 1932. A heap of charred rubble is all that is left of a cobblers shop following a fire and gas explosion which killed Station Officer Mark Eady of Strand Road Fire Station and injured fourteen others. The occupier, Walter Stevenson, his wife and two daughters, who were asleep in the flat above when the fire started, escaped uninjured.

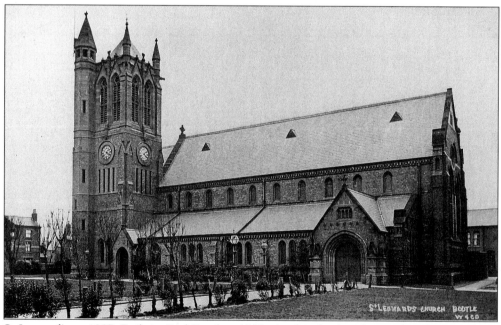

St Leonard's, c. 1907. Built in Peel Road in 1889, this lovely church stayed with us until the May blitz, when it was bombed and destroyed. A new St Leonard's has been built on the same site.

St Leonard's, c. 1911. This interior view shows the pulpit, pews, arches, windows and wrought ironwork of this beautiful church.

Rimrose Gardens, 1908. This rare photograph was taken during the opening ceremony by Mayor George Randell, in Peel Road, on 3 June 1908. Top left is St Joans School with Hemans Street in the background.

St Winifrides, *c.* 1904, built originally as a Methodist church before becoming a Catholic church, at the junction of Rimrose Road and Church Street. It was closed in 1956 when a new church was built on the Oriel Road and Merton Road corner.

Cranworth Street, *c.* 1900. This beautiful row of terraced houses off Rimrose Road, running parallel with Grove Street, is now long gone. The Rimrose estate now occupies this location. This estate is now due for demolition and a new housing estate is to be built here. 'X' marks the house of Peter McIntyre.

Boswell Street looking up towards Peel Road, 1907. The grocers shop of Jackson Jones is seen left and the bakers of William Harrison is on the other corner. Local children at play complete the picture.

Knowsley Road, c. 1930. A view looking up Knowsley Road, towards Gray Street, with Bowles Street to the left, during a St Leonard's Church Walk of Witness. Two trams have come to a standstill as the walk comes out of Gray Street.

Dryden Street, c. 1910, from Knowsley Road, looking towards Peel Road. The delivery cart near the top of the street has Carr's Malt Bread and Cakes on it.

Knowsley Road, c. 1953. A 61 route single-deck, six-wheeled bus, registration number KF 1037, on it way to Aigburth Vale, stops to pick up passengers outside the Gainsboro Picture House. Just out of view on the left would be the Empire Picture Palace. J. Maudsley was the manager. Behind the bus is the Bankhall Mission Hall, and on the other corner is G.H. Parry & Sons Ltd, bakers.

Knowsley Road, *c.* 1970. The King George VI Club was built in 1956 near to the junction with Hornby Boulevard. It is used by local senior citizens for various functions. It closed for a while and reopened on 29 May 1987.

Stanley Road, 1904. St Matthew's church was established in 1887 and the new church opened in 1891. It could accommodate 600 persons and is at the junction with Hornby Road. The vicarage is to the left of the church.

St Matthew's *c.* 1914. This photograph of the interior of this beautiful church, with arches running the entire length, was taken by W. & Co.

St Matthew's, *c.* 1920. This group photograph shows the church hockey club of St Matthew's, Stanley Road. The club was made up of parishioners, seen here with the vicar.

Stanley Road, c. 1951. The St Matthew's Church Lads Brigade marching to a church service, escorted by a Bootle Borough police constable, just passing North Park. The Bootle Health Centre and Johnsons Dyers are in the distance.

Stanley Road, 1905. The funeral procession of Father Nugent, a Catholic priest, passes along Stanley Road past its junction with Knowsley Road, on its way to Ford cemetery, 30 June 1905. Along with Mayor Lester, Father Nugent took in homeless children, and has done more in Liverpool than anyone else to bring Catholics and Protestants together.

Stanley Road, *c.* 1948. A lone Bootle bobby stands at the junction of Stanley Road and Knowsley Road on school crossing duty. On the opposite corner of Linacre Lane is Martin's Bank. Note that the tram lines intersect the roundabout.

Stanley Road, *c.* 1902. This postcard is incorrectly titled Linacre Road. On the corner of Linacre Lane is the Liverpool Savings Bank. Next door is the sub-post office and stationers run by Miss Alice Morgan, a confectioners run by William Cropper and the chemists of Granville E. Paddock.

Stanley Road, c. 1912. The premises of Johnsons, dyers and cleaners, was established in Mildmay Road, Bootle in 1817. The house on the corner was eventually demolished for the extensions to the works. Some of the workers can be seen on a fire escape, having a break.

Stanley Road, c. 1918. Johnson Brothers (Dyers) Ltd, Bootle Dye Works. This interior shot shows the curtain finishing department. This postcard was an official Johnsons reply card. It states on the reverse side, 'Dear Madam, We Have Pleasure In Informing You That Your Order Is Now Ready.'

Foundation stone, *c.* 1910. This was laid at St Andrew's church prior to the completion of the church hall in St Andrew's Road on the opposite corner to the church.

Stanley Road, *c.* 1915. This aerial view, taken from the top of the Johnsons water tower, shows St Andrew's church, church hall, and St Andrew's Road, with Litherland Road running parallel with Stanley Road. The Melaneer factory and its chimneys are just visible.

Litherland Road, c. 1850. Another artist's impression of early Bootle, this time of some farm cottages in Litherland Road. They are believed to have been just behind Johnsons recreation grounds.

LINACRE LANE
1883

Linacre Lane, c. 1883. Returning back along Stanley Road, we turn left up Linacre Lane. This view is taken from a painting, though how accurate it is we do not know. There are farm buildings on the left, where Linacre School now stands; the lane leading up to the canal bridge.

Linacre village, 1896. This is the earliest photograph taken by W.&Co. in my collection. It shows Linacre Lane and the Linacre pub, which was re-erected in 1882 after the roof of the original pub was removed and a new pub built on top of it. After the present road was constructed the original pub entrance was below ground level and was subject to flooding, so it was re-erected. On the corner of Litherland Road was Websters general store, and next door but one was the house belonging to a Mrs Holland. These houses were demolished to make way for the Bootle Gas Works.

William Harvey Ltd., c. 1930. Part of the 'Calcine' department. The raw ore from either Bolivia or Argentina was brought in, 'Calcined' and roasted. This turned it into a light brown sandy mixture ready for the furnaces. Three of the Calcine furnaces can be seen in the background. Two men are pushing the calcined material across the yard to the main furnaces.

William Harvey Ltd., *c.* 1929. This superb photograph shows G.T.C. lorry registration number EM 1382 belonging to the Mellanear Works, Lunt Road, Bootle. The driver could be Ted Spedding. On the lorry are bags of Bolivian ore; more bags are stacked in the yard.

William Harvey Ltd, *c.* 1920. William Rimmer (left) and Wilson Hayes sweat it out in the blacksmiths shop inside this well-known Bootle factory.

William Harvey Ltd, *c.* 1930, showing the Metal Store and the stacks of tin ingots, each weighing 100lb. They are ready to be taken by lorry to the docks for shipment to all parts of the world. The foreman (in the suit) is Ernie Merryfield.

James Baxendale photographed in Aintree Road, not far from where the roundabout would be, *c.* 1913. Jim, who had his yard nearby, is seen here with his horse 'Poppy'. Walton Prison can be seen in the distance.

Royal visit, c. 1942, not long after the May blitz, one of the many royal visits to the borough. Their Majesties King George VI and Queen Elizabeth are accompanied by the Bootle County Borough Constabulary along the passageway at the rear of Monfa Road, between Kirby Road and Ainsdale Road. The church of St John and St James is the background.

Hawthorne Road Council School, c. 1911. School teacher Miss Bessie Lewis is seen with group 5. Only two of the pupils have been identified: back row, third and fourth from left are sisters Madge and Nell. Their surname is not known.

Gloucester Road, *c.* 1926, taken from Earl Road looking towards Aintree Road. Hawthorne Road Council School is on the left near Aintree Road. Note the massive telegraph poles.

Worcester Road, *c.* 1926, tree-lined, traffic- and litter-free, taken from Oxford Road. The Derby Park railings are to the right. Aintree Road is just visible at the far end.

Derby Road, *c.* 1924. Multiview of the park, with sixteen scenes, mainly of the lake, but including some features which no longer exist, such as the aviary, conservatories, summer houses. Many will remember the lake.

Oxford Road entrance to Derby Park, *c.* 1903, showing the beautiful ornate gates that were presented to the citizens of Bootle by Lord Derby, along with the park which was opened to the public in 1895. The house inside the park was the home of head gardener Mr Drysdale according to the note at the bottom of this postcard.

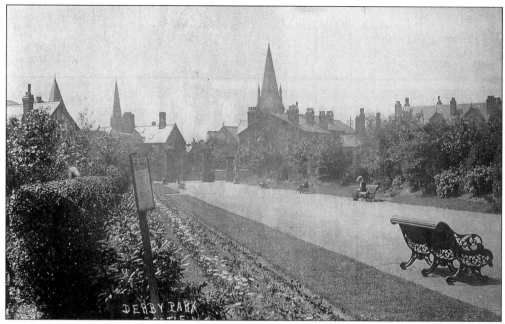

A tranquil scene, Derby Park, *c*. 1904. Local residents are enjoying a sit down on a park seat near to the Oxford Road entrance. The two spires belong to Trinity church and Christ Church. The notice on top of the post is headed 'Theft and Misuse of Shrubs and Plants'. They had their problems in those days too!

Derby Park, *c*. 1905. In its heyday Derby Park boasted two long greenhouses, in which the majority of the plants and shrubs in the park were grown.

Derby Park, *c.* 1924. The balustrade, steps and summer houses were one of the lovely features of this park. The beautiful lawns and flower beds were a credit to the gardener. In later years the summerhouse was turned into storage sheds which were eventually vandalized.

Derby Park, *c.* 1918. At the end of World War One the Mayor, Harry Pennington, Mayoress and other civic dignitaries had a reception in Derby Park, where they entertained widows, relatives and friends of Bootle's fallen heroes. As the Mayor met each one the band played on the bandstand.

Derby Park, *c.* 1910. Bootle's famous lake and rustic bridge. Many a happy hour was spent by Bootle families playing on the lake. I wonder how many children fell in or were pushed into the lake? Swans swam on it, although they are not shown here.

Derby Park Lake (*c.* 1907) was very popular with local model yacht clubs as well of those from further afield, who used to race their boats here. Alas, the lake is no more, although its contours are still visible in the park.

Derby Park, *c.* 1912. This view, looking towards Earl Road, shows the bandstand in the centre of the pathway. In the distance can be seen Walton Prison, which was built in 1855 to replace Kirkdale Jail.

Christmas postcard, *c.* 1910. A typical seasons greeting produced by local photographers at the turn of the century. This card comprises three different photographs of the family of Charles Williams (shipwright), his wife and son. They resided at 30 Alt Road, Bootle. The photographer was R.B. Churchyard of Fazakerly.

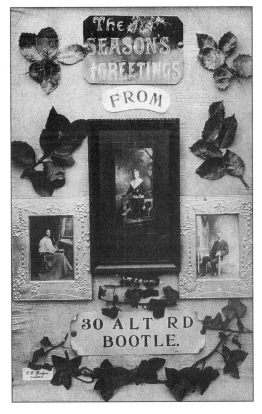

Orriel School, *c.* 1916, boys department, Standard 4. This school, at the junction of Sefton Road and Aughton Road, was built in 1910 and had accommodation for 1,200. In charge of the boys was W.F. Towndrow, the girls Miss A. Peake, and the infants Miss E. Kay.

Foundation stone, *c.* 1910. This was laid at the church of St John and St James, Monfa Road, on the Klondyke estate. The houses in the background could be part of Menai Road.

Leonard Tennant, *c.* 1918. Along with his first wife Becky, he was the first resident on the Klondyke estate in Province Road, Bootle. Leonard is seen outside his home at No. 17, proudly wearing the uniform of a railway goods guard.

Leonard Tennant (*c.* 1912) was a goods guard for the Lancashire and Yorkshire Railway. He is seen with another railway man with his own guards van which has his name on it. He is holding a piece of his equipment for uncoupling and coupling wagons. The photograph is thought to have been taken in the goods yard at the rear of Bootle Hospital.

St George of England School concert in the school hall, 1950-51. The choir was from the nearby Roberts Secondary School. The all-girl choir was assisted by parents and teachers. The head of Roberts School was Miss A. Adams, and of St George was Mr Fletcher.

Roberts Drive School, c. 1949. A smiling group of pupils poses for the school photographer in the school grounds. None of them is identified, but perhaps someone will recognise themselves and let me know?

Corporation Hospital, 1904. Its full title was the Bootle Corporation Hospital for Infectious Diseases and it was situated at the junction of Linacre Lane and Fernhill Road, covering land which now forms part of the Fernhill Sports Centre and part of the school fields for St George of England School. Its Medical Superintendent was W.A. Daly MD, BS, BSc (Lon); Resident Medical Officer was W. Paton Phillips MB, Ch.B, and the Matron was a Miss Johnson. It had 120 beds.

Mary Road, 192, a typical side street with terraced type housing, photographed from Cinder Lane, looking towards Springwell Road.

Cinder Lane, *c.* 1926. The crowning of a local church May Queen. Who the queen was or from which church is not known. The nearest church was St John and St James. The houses to the rear are either Cinder Lane or Hermitage Grove.

Cinder Lane, *c.* 1920. This young lad is believed to be David, the son of Samuel Williams of Walnut Cottage (almost the site of the present Walnut public house). David is playing in his 'Tad-Sad' pedal car in Cinder Lane. His clothes, fur gloves and pedal car suggest that his parents were rather well-to-do.

St Robert Bellarmine's, 1934. At the junction of Harris Drive and Orrel Road, Bootle, stands this Roman Catholic church. It was built in 1934 to replace the Stable Church.

The Stable Church, c. 1932. At the rear of 24 Alexander Drive, Bootle was an old stable which was converted into a temporary Catholic church when Fr Robert Coupe was chosen to establish a new parish in the area and the only premises available were the stable. This postcard shows the exterior and main entrance.

The Stable Church, *c.* 1932. The interior measured just seven paces in length and four paces in width providing just enough room for thirty persons at a time. The Stable Church was closed when the new church of St Robert Bellarmine was opened. The lower half of this altar is still in use in the school hall.

St Robert Bellarmine church, 1933. The laying of the foundation stone was performed by Archbishop Downey, Bishop of Liverpool, on 17 September 1933. The church was built on land once owned by the Walker family (Walkers Tannery) and by Threlfalls Brewery, and was opened by Bishop Dobson on 11 December 1934.

St Robert Bellarmine, c. 1934. The architect was Pritchards, the builders were the firm of John Williams (Liverpool) Ltd, and the cost was £11,115 9s 2d. It can accommodate approximately 500 persons. Its present priest is Father Edward Cain.

Patrick Avenue, Bootle, c. 1945. The street party to celebrate VJ Day, one of many all over Bootle, photographed outside 48 Patrick Avenue. A few of these children still live in Patrick Avenue to this day.

Patrick Avenue, Bootle, c. 1945. The adults had a lot to be thankful for and celebrated with their children. They included the families of Chadwick, Steel, Mann, Coskayne, Chorley, Finney, Hayes, Wilson, Neial, Curtis, Beatty, Cropper, Mawdesley, Oldfield, Williams, Eastwood, Addicott, Kelly, Aldrich, Cambell and Alcock.

Four
Bootle Borough Police

Bootle-cum-Linacre was policed by Lancashire County Police Force until 1887, when Bootle County Borough Police was formed. As the new force had no cells of its own, they rented them from Lancashire at a cost of £40 per year. The force's main station was at 2 Derby Road, next to the toll gate. The building was a dwelling house owned by the Police Surgeon, a Dr Sprakeling, who was retained at a cost of £52 per annum. It was used mainly as offices and single men's quarters.

The Old Court House, c. 1887. This building adjoining the police station fronted onto Strand Road. The Borough Police Court was built in 1881. The 'Bridewell' of this building was used at one point as a police station; it was situated below the court and reached by way of steps from pavement level in Strand Road. The police station and court house are long gone.

Mann Street Police Station, *c*. 1891. A police sub-station was opened in 1891 at 1-3 Mann Street, off Derby Road. It was in fact two dwelling houses converted into one. The entrance was through the vestibule door (left) into the Bridewell, which consisted of a wooden counter and desk. A door led off to two cells. Police Inspector Benson and his wife had the living part of the station. The policemen standing outside Mann Street are, left to right: Sgt 18 Schofield, PC 41 Robert Smith, Sgt 29 Whelan and PC 31 Harry Irosen.

Oriel Road, Bridewell, *c*. 1930. This fine building was built in 1891, complete with Magistrates Court, at a cost of £13,096. It was the headquarters of Bootle Borough Police Force and it had ten cells, a police drill yard, van house, stables for two horses, dormitory accommodation for fifteen constables, a bridewell, and drying rooms, lockers and, later, a police social club in the basement.

The main entrance to Bootle Police Station, just off Orriel Road, 1960. This was the entrance for the public and prisoners alike. When prisoners arrived in a police vehicle two iron gates closed behind them to prevent any escape attempt.

A Bootle 'Bobby', c. 1915. Police Sergeant 50 J.W. Scott was photographed at the rear of his home at 5 Norton Street, Bootle, proudly wearing his Long Service and Good Conduct Medal, with three bars and a red and white ribbon. He is wearing a light coloured helmet. This was his summer weight issue, made of compressed straw for lightness and comfort. It is a far cry form the helmets the modern force wear today. They are heavier and uncomfortable to wear. Sgt Scott most probably joined the force at its formation in 1887.

Police Constable No. 6, c. 1926. William L. Alcock was a Bootle Borough constable under P.T. Browne, Chief Constable between 1920 and 1926. PC Alcock lived at 113 Fernhill Road, Bootle. He was photographed in a local studio wearing his police and military medals. Notice the spiked helmet.

Opposite: This is one of the many police boxes scattered around the borough, c. 1930. This one was at the junction of Peel Road and Rimrose Road. A constable is taking down a young lady's particulars, watched by his Inspector and a motor cycle patrol. The registration number of the motor cycle is EM 2274.

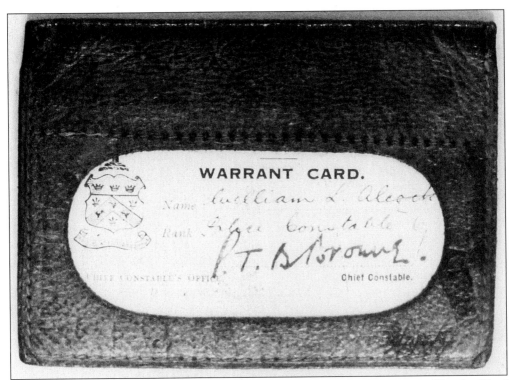

Police Warrant Card, *c.* 1926. This is the warrant card of PC Alcock. It is signed by the Chief Constable and has the Bootle coat of arms on it.

Long Service Medals, 1942. HM Inspector of Constabularies is seen with members of Bootle Police. Left to right, back row: PC Cottier, Sgt Whiteman, Insp. Moir, Sgt Dobson, PC Cairns. Front row: PC Scott, Chief Insp Ross (HMI), Chief Constable Tom Bell, Sgt Forshaw and PC McCarthy.

Group photo, *c.* 1940. Police Sergeant 20, Eric Graves, is photographed outside the entrance to Oriel Road Bridewell with, left to right: Inspector Grant, War Reserve Welsh and Constable Bill Slowey.

Force Inspection, 1950. Members of Bootle Borough Police being inspected by HM Inspector of Constabulary Major J. Egan, accompanied by Chief Inspector W.E. Pitts and the Mayor of Bootle, C.G. Anderson. Police officers identified include PC A. Jones, PC K. Poole, PC J. Jones, PC B. Ellery, PC S. Oakman. The photograph was taken in the rear yard of Oriel Road Bridewell.

Opposite: Bootle Police Club, 1972. Bootle Borough Police Force amalgamated with Liverpool City Police to form Liverpool and Bootle Constabulary in 1967, which became Merseyside Police in 1972. This photograph was taken in the Bootle Police Club, in the basement of Oriel Road Bridewell, on its last night. Left to right: N. Hart, Jim Ruxton (barman), H. Jones, Ted Platt (Clerk to Court), C. Aindow (Special), D. Gilliland, -?-, H. Legge (Chief Constable), F. Rooney, Jean Bell (daughter of ex-Chief Constable Tom Bell), T. McCarthy, W, James (war reserve), H. Owens, B. Gilbertson, W. Woods.

Police v Wyndham Hotel, 1953. A bowls match was held on a regular basis between these two teams. Not all here have been identified. Back row: Harry 'Gunner' Gill (Bootle Cricket Club), B. Rogerson, Ald. Kelly, B. Spurling, E. Graves, B. Gilbertson, C. Pearson, B. Jack, B. Brown (Lic. Wyndham), D. Bolton (civilian), A. Hector. Front row: two unknown Specials, J. Baillie, B. Brown, B. Gerrard, F. Holt, D. Shackleton, H. Owens, W. James.

Police Constable 2481 Woolley, 1975, the author of this book, sitting in his 'Panda' car outside the New Strand, Bootle. Peter Woolley joined Bootle Borough Police in 1965 and saw service all over Bootle, including the Docks. He served in Liverpool City Centre until he retired on medical grounds in 1992.

Five

Bootle May Day Demonstration

Bootle's first May Day was held in 1896, succeeding the decorated cycle parades which had been held some years previously. The first May Queen was Alice Parry. The celebration took the form of a procession around the Borough, culminating in the crowning and other events in North Park. The success of the first show proved that the people would give it their full support in the future. The event was staged over three days. It continued until World War One, when it was suspended between 1916 and 1919, and in 1940 it was decided to suspend it again. By 1945, however, many of the committee had left the district having lost their homes and others had died and the committee was wound up. Because of Miss May Logan's love of Bootle and the May Days, a new committee was formed, and the event became known as Bootle Carnival. This continued until 1966, but the event was losing money, and poor attendances caused it to be finally abandoned.

Bootle's first May Queen, 1896. Miss Alice Parry, aged twelve years, was Bootle May Demonstration's first queen. She was the daughter of Mr W.H. Parry, the May Day Committee Chairman.

Ruth Sanders, 1906, photographed after being crowned with her retinue in North Park. The crowning was performed by the Mayor of Bootle, Robert E. Roberts.

Bootle May Day, 1906. This horse-drawn fire engine is at the junction of Strand Road with Washington Street during the procession. Strand Road railway station bridge is in the background. The shops include The Climax Boot Company and Davies Son & Co., Strand Road Market.

Bootle May Day, 1906. One of the many schools taking part was Hawthorne Road Council School. In the background another float moves down Hornby Road prior to entering North Park. The float was loaned by Crawfords Delightful Biscuits.

Bootle May Day, 1907. Kathleen Miller wearing her beautiful dress in the studio of W. & Co., after being crowned.

Bootle May Day, 1907. The procession has come to a standstill in Stanley Road, near to the canal bridge. Not only did this give the horses a rest but it gave the cameraman time to take this super shot. The first team are unknown; the second belonged to the Bootle Coke Company, Marsh Lane. Shops include Hanley Pottery Stores, George Dimler, John Irwins, and The Parisian Studios. The Langton Hotel can be seen further down.

The Bootle Morris Dancers warming up in a rear garden of a house in Merton Road, prior to joining the parade. Their trainer was a Mr Starkey, and he can just be seen in the background in the straw cadie.

Bootle May Day, 1907. It was not all work for the Bootle Fire Brigade; they liked to let their hair down too. On this occasion they are the 'Blacko' Fire Brigade, posing near to the Leeds and Liverpool Canal.

Bootle May Day, 1907. Another well-loved dancing troupe was 'The Alhabama Coons', an all-boy troop. Even the 'girls' were boys dressed up. Their trainer was also Mr Starkey. The whole troupe pose in North Park.

Bootle May Day, 1908. This was the year of Mary Agnes Dunne, who is just about to leave the Town Hall to join the procession in her lovely carriage. This postcard was given out as an advertisement for a Mr Scholefield, JP and shipowner.

Bootle May Day, 1910. Miss Mabel Thomas poses in the studio of Wright & Co., Stanley Road. Notice that her hair is in ringlets. It was stipulated that no queen could have straight hair.

WITH
Mr. & Mrs. H. COLEMAN'S
COMPLIMENTS.

Bootle
May-Day Demonstratio
1910.

Bootle May Day, 1910. A complimentary postcard was given away by a Mr and Mrs Coleman, licenced victualars of the Bootle Arms Hotel, 5 Derby Road. Mable Thomas is seen with Bootle's Mayor, Harry Carruthers and members of the committee.

Bootle May Day, 1911. Violet Wilson, the daughter of Mr J. Wilson, solicitor and Deputy Town Clerk, was the 1911 May Queen. She stands proudly as her official photograph is taken.

Bootle May Day, 1911. Third prize winner in Class 5 was the rig entered by Mr Enos Wood, team owner, contractor and coal merchant of 2-4 Thornton Road. Here he shows off to his family outside his home.

Bootle May Day, 1913. Miss Ella Phipps resplendent in her gown and train, complete with a large bouquet of flowers and looking slightly nervous, poses for the camera.

Bootle May Day, 1914. Janet Lamb, with an absolutely beautiful train, was chosen for that year's May Queen.

Bootle May Day, 1919, the first May Day celebration following the end of the First World War. Years 1916-18 were cancelled. Jessie Coleman, Queen that year, was known as the 'Peace' Queen. She is seen in her back garden posing for the camera of Percival Sutcliffe.

Bootle May Day, 1920. Bootle's own 'Alhabama Coons' in relaxed mood, showing off their costumes. What a pity they did not have colour photography in those days!

BOOTLE MAY QUEEN (MISS NORA COLLINGS) AND RETINUE, JUNE 1923. *Photo* FOULDS & HIBBERD

Bootle May Day, 1923. Miss Nora Collings and her retinue pose for the camera of Foulds & Hibberds of Seaforth. It includes the Dowager Queen, Miss Vida Carr.

Bootle May Day, 1924, May Day Demonstration 'Jubilee' year, when Miss Jean Pilkington was chosen as May Queen. She was the daughter of Tom Pilkington, who was on the finance committees, and Mrs Pilkington, who was the directress of the Jubilee Café.

Bootle May Day, 1926. One of the main events in the main area was the judging of the working horses. The gentleman second left is Mr Summers, a local and highly respected veterinary surgeon in Bootle. Also in the photograph is a Mr Rimmer and his horse.

Bootle May Day, 1931. Miss Phyllis Spence, wearing a tiara, in the studios of Terence Ridgeway of Knowsley Road. The train is about the longest one we have seen.

Bootle May Day, 1931. Miss Edna May Fairweather was a nice young lady and made a lovely May Queen. Wearing her tiara over her ringlets, she is photographed by Terence Ridgeway. She died in 1988.

Bootle May Day, 1932. One of the marching bands that were a favourite with the crowds that lined the route. This was the LMSR (London Midland Scottish Railway) 'Prize' Jazz Band. Their motto was 'We Lead, Others Follow'. They are shown in Knowsley Road.

Bootle May Day, 1936. Miss Coralie Crocket poses with her retinue in North Park for one of the official photographs. This was one of the most successful May Days for many years according to the BMDD chairman, Mr J.T. Warburton. The May Queen was crowned by the Mayor of Bootle, John W. Clarke.

Bootle May Day, 1940, the last May Day Demonstration before the Second World War took hold. Miss Niana Mills is seen with her Dowager Queen Jean McKenzie. They are sitting in a carriage outside Bootle Town Hall. Note the sand-bags piled up around the walls.

Acknowledgements

I would like to thank the following who have assisted me in compiling this volume, by loaning photographs and offering information. Others wished to remain anonymous. I apologise to those I have omitted to mention.

Mrs Baxendale, Charles Bedford, Mrs Bilsborough, Paul Bolger, Fr Edward Cain, Colour Copy Centre, Liverpool, Mr Davis, Mrs Ethel Evans, Jim O'Neil, Bob Rimmer, Jack Rimmer, John Roles, John Ryan

This book is dedicated to my wife Patricia